Health Lesson 7

D1524724

The Spleen

SonLight Education Ministry
United States of America

A Suggested Daily Schedule

(Adapt this schedule to your family needs.)

5:00 a.m.   Arise–Personal Worship

6:00 a.m.   Family Worship and Bible Class–With Father

7:00 a.m.   Breakfast

8:00 a.m.   Practical Arts*–Domestic Activities
                     Agriculture
                     Industrial Arts
                     (especially those related to
                     the School Lessons)

10:00 a.m.   School Lessons
              (Take a break for some physical exercise
              during this time slot.)

12:00 p.m.   Dinner Preparations
              (Health class could be included at this time
              or a continued story.)

1:00 p.m.   Dinner

2:00 p.m.   Practical Arts* or Fine Arts
              (Music and Crafts)
              (especially those related to
              the School Lessons)

5:00 p.m.   Supper

6:00 p.m.   Family Worship–Father
              (Could do History Class)

7:00 p.m.   Personal time with God–Bed Preparation

8:00 p.m.   Bed

*Daily nature walk can be in morning or afternoon.

The Desire of All Nations

This book is a part of a curriculum that is built upon the life of Christ entitled, "The Desire of All Nations," for grades 2-8. Any of the books in this curriculum can be used by themselves or as an entire program.

INFORMATION ABOUT THE 2-8 GRADE PROGRAM

Multi-level

This program is written on a multi-level. That means that each booklet has material for grades 2-8. This is so the whole family in these grades may work from the same books. It is difficult for a busy mother to have 2 or more children and each have a different set of books. Remember, the Bible is written for all ages.

The Bible—the Primary Textbook

The books in this program are designed to teach the parent and the student how to learn academic subjects by using the Bible as a primary textbook.

The Desire of Ages

The Desire of Ages by Ellen G. White is used as a textbook to go with the Bible. This focuses on the early life of Christ, when He was a child. Children relate best to Christ as a child and youth.

Lesson Numbers

The big number in the top right corner on the cover of this book is the Lesson Number and corresponds with the chapter number in the book *The Desire of Ages*. For example, Lesson 1 in the school program will go along with chapter 1 in *The Desire of Ages*. Usually each family starts at the beginning with Lesson 1. Most children have not had a true Bible program, therefore they need the foundation built. If there is academic material that they have already covered, they do the Bible part and review then pass quickly on.

Seven Academic Subjects

There are seven academic subjects in this program—Health, Mathematics, Music, Science–Nature, History/Geography/Prophecy, Language, Voice–Speech.

Language Program

A good, solid language program is recommended to be used along with the SonLight materials.

The Riggs Institute has a multi-sensory teaching method that accommodates every child's unique learning style. Their program is called *Writing and Spelling Road to Reading and Thinking*. Order by calling (800) 200-4840 or visit www.riggsinst.org. (Disclaimer: SonLight does not endorse the reading books recommended in the Riggs' program.)

Another option which you might find more user friendly and is similar to the Riggs program but from a Christian perspective is *Spell to Write and Read* by Wanda Sanseri. To order, call Wanda Sanseri at (503) 654-2300 or visit https://www.bhibooks.net/swr.html

"Childhood of Jesus"
Lesson 7 – Truthfulness

The following books are those you will need for this lesson.
All of these can be obtained from www.sonlighteducation.com

The Rainbow Covenant – Study the spiritual meaning of colors and make your own rainbow book.

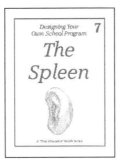

Health
The Spleen

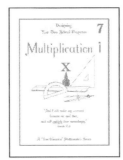

Math
Multiplication I

Music
The Half, Quarter and Eighth Notes and Rest

Science/Nature
Review Astronomy

A Casket – Coloring book and story. Learn how to treat the gems of the Bible.

H/G/P
Australia

Language
Pure Words

Speech/Voice
Correct Bodily Alignment

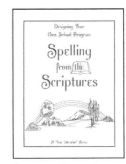

Spelling from the Scriptures

Bible Study – Learn how to study the Bible and helpful use tools.

Bible
*The Desire of all Nations II
Teacher Study Guide*

Student Study Guide

Bible Lesson Study Guide

Memory Verses
*The Desire of all Nations II
Scripture Songs Book*

and MP3 files

Our Nature Study Book – Your personal nature journal.

Table of Contents

Truthfulness

Truthfulness and integrity
are attributes of God,
and he who possesses
these qualities
possesses a power
that is invincible.
Never prevaricate;
never tell an untruth
in precept or in example.
Be straight and undeviating.
Even a slight prevarication
should not be allowed.

Teacher Section

*"Give,
and it shall be given unto you;
good measure...
and running over."*
Luke 6:38

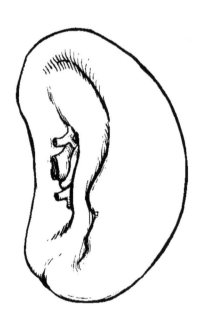

INSTRUCTIONS
For the Teacher

Step 1

Study the Bible Lesson and begin to memorize the Memory Verses. Familiarize yourself with the Character Quality.

The student can answer the Bible Review Questions. See page 6. Use the Steps in Bible Study.

Bible Lesson

Childhood of Jesus – Luke 2:39-40

Memory Verses

Luke 2:39-40; Luke 2:51-52; Acts 17:27; John 9:4; Isaiah 42:1-4; Proverbs 20:11

Character Quality

Truthfulness – Honesty, straight forwardness, the quality of being **true** to principle, or corresponding with fact or reality.

Antonyms – <u>Untruthfulness</u>; lying; falsehood; deceptiveness

Character Quality Verse

Ephesians 4:25 – *"Wherefore putting away lying, speak every man **truth** with his neighbour: for we are members one of another."*

Step 2

Understand How To/And

A. Do the spelling cards so the student can begin to build his own spiritual dictionary.

B. Mark the Bible.

C. Evaluate your student's character in relation to the character quality of **truthfulness**.

D. Familiarize yourself with the spleen, and how it works. Notice the projects.

E. Review the Scripture References for "**Truthfulness.**"

F. Notice the Answer Key.

A. Spelling Cards

Spelling Lists

Health Words
Place I - II - III
clots
filter
flow
generous
heart
obscure
purple
serve
spleen
storage

Place II - III
antibodies
circulating
delicate
emergency
function
immune system
infection
policemen
sieve

Place III
bone marrow
coagulated

Bible Words
filled
Galilee
grace
grew
increase
learned
letters
Nazareth
Rabbi
spirit
strong
subject
truthfulness
waxed

Place III cont.
circulatory
      system
lymphocytes
macrophages
sinusoids
reconstruct
splenic artery
transfusion
vegetarian
      or vegan

> See the booklet
> *Spelling from the Scriptures*
> for instructions about how to make
> the Spelling Cards.

B. How to Mark the Bible

1. Copy the list of Bible texts in the back of the Bible on an empty page as a guide.

2. Go to the first text in the Bible and copy the next text beside it. Go to the next one and repeat the process until they are all chain-referenced.

3. Have the student present the study to family and/or friends.

4. Each student lesson contains one or more sections that have a Bible marking study on the subject studied. (See the student's section, page 35.)

C. Evaluate Your Student's Character

This section is for the purpose of helping the teacher know how to encourage the students to become more **truthful**.

See page 7.

> **Place I = Grades 2-3-4**
> **Place II = Grades 4-5-6**
> **Place III = Grades 6-7-8**

D. Familiarize Yourself With How the Spleen Works – Notice the Projects

Projects

1. Read a book about angels. Remember how the invisible angels care for us like the white blood cells do in their sphere. Satan can remind us of bacteria, that would like to destroy us.

2. Take a nature walk and answer the question: How do plants protect themselves from harmful things that seek to destroy them? (This might require a little more study.)

3. Observe a water filter to better understand the job of the spleen. Change air conditioning or heating filters. Father can explain the importance of the oil filter when he changes it in the car.

4. Play a game of hide-and-go-seek. Think of how the spleen is tucked away in an obscure place, and so was boy Jesus during His childhood years.

5. Dry, freeze, or can some food as a physical analogy about how the spleen stores extra red blood cells.

6. Visit a blood bank. Learn about how the blood is processed.

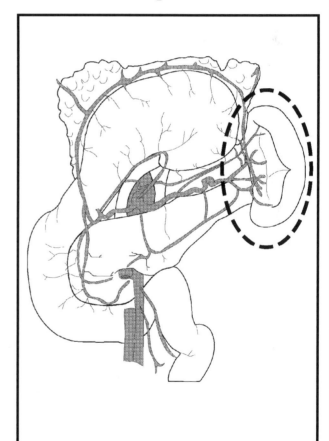

Remember,
God has a purpose for every part of the body.
He has a purpose for your life.
Do you understand it?

E. Review the Scripture References for "Truthfulness"

Teacher, read through this section before working on the lesson with the student.

See page 35 of the student section.

F. Notice the Answer Key

The answer key for the student book is found on page 8.

Step 3

Read the Lesson Aim.

Lesson Aim

The aim of this lesson is to teach the student about the spleen and its function. Teach the child that God has a purpose for every part of the body. Boy Jesus served a purpose in His home as He demonstrated **truthfulness**.

The spleen is a soft, purplish-colored organ found behind and to the left of the stomach. A human spleen is about the size of a fist. (Much is not known yet about the spleen.) The spleen has an important part to play, in the digestive system, circulatory system, and in the immune system. The spleen is important because:

First, the body stores extra red blood cells in the spleen. The spleen releases these whenever the body needs extra blood.

Second, the spleen helps filter useless substances from the blood. Blood passing through the spleen travels through a maze of sponge-like spaces (sinusoids). There, large cells (macrophages) surround and destroy old or damaged blood cells.

Third, the spleen helps the body fight infection. (Macrophages rid the blood of certain parasites and bacteria.) The spleen contains clumps of white blood cells (lymphocytes) which release special proteins into the blood. These proteins (antibodies) weaken or kill bacteria, viruses, and other infectious substances.

In a similar way, we learn these spiritual lessons:

(1) By studying and living by God's Word, we can rid our lives of old

damaging ways like the spleen helps filter useless substances from the body. Lying is one thing we want to be rid of because we want to follow the example of Jesus and live a **truthful** life.

(2) In order to preserve itself the spleen contains lymphocytes which are constantly on guard against infectious substances. Jesus was constantly on guard in order to preserve His purity. He was subject to all the conflicts which we have to meet, that He might be an example to us in childhood, youth, and manhood. He lived a life of purity, and practiced **truthfulness** in everything He did each day. Do you follow Jesus' example?

(3) Satan was lurking around like a disease germ in the body, unwearied in his efforts to overcome the Child, the youth, and the man of Nazareth. From His earliest years, Jesus was guarded by heavenly angels which can remind us of the white blood cells, yet His life was one long struggle against the powers of evil. He was wise to discern evil, and strong to resist it.

Step 4

Prepare to begin the Spleen Lesson.

To Begin the Spleen Lesson

As an introduction to the lesson, it will be helpful if the teacher hides and has the children find her. Then tell them, "there is an organ in the body that is located in a rather hidden place; it is the spleen. Can you find it?" (Present an anatomy chart for the student to look at.)

Another possible way to introduce this lesson is to plan a closet-cleaning project. As you go through the items and sort them to be discarded, recycled, or donated to some charity, tell the students there is a storage closet in the body temple where sorting is carried on. Ask them to guess what organ sorts over all the red blood cells as they pass through and takes all that are not normal or healthy out of circulation. (For a hint you could use the following little rhyme and let them guess the last word.)
   This organ can't be seen
   But its name is the <u>spleen</u>.

Step 5

Begin the Spleen Lesson. Cover only what can be understood by your student. Make the lessons a family project by all being in-

volved in part or all of the lesson. These lessons are designed for the whole family.

Steps in Bible Study

1. Prayer

2. Read the verses/meditate/memorize.

3. Look up key words in Strong's Concordance and find their meanings in the Hebrew or Greek dictionary in the back of that book.

4. Cross reference (marginal reference) with other Bible texts. An excellent study tool is The Treasury of Scripture Knowledge.

5. Use Bible custom books for more information on the times.

6. Write a summary of what you have learned from those verses.

7. Mark key thoughts in the margin of your Bible.

8. Share your study with others to reinforce the lessons you have learned.

Review Questions

1. Where did Jesus live in His childhood? (Luke 2:39)

2. Did He grow as other children grow? (Luke 2:40)

3. With what was He filled? What was upon Him? (Luke 2:40)

4. By whom were Jewish children educated in the days of Christ? (Luke 2:46)

5. Was He educated in the schools of the rabbis? (John 7:15)

6. Who was His first human teacher? (His mother)

7. What do His teachings show as to His knowledge of Scripture, and of nature? (He had studied the Scriptures and nature.)

8. What was the moral influence of Nazareth? (John 1:46) Had it any effect upon Him? (II Corinthians 5:21)

9. Explain what it means that Jesus:

"Waxed strong in spirit," and was *"filled with wisdom."*

Evaluating Your Child's Character

Check the appropriate box for your student's level of development,
or your own, as the case may be.

Maturing Nicely (MN), Needs Improvement (NI), Poorly Developed (PD), Absent (A)

Truthfulness

1. Does the child report accidents and damage immediately?

MN   NI   PD   A
❑   ❑   ❑   ❑

2. Does the child rationalize or cover up wrong behavior?

Yes   No
❑   ❑

3. Can the child's word be counted upon?

Yes   No
❑   ❑

4. Does the child state things accurately, without exaggeration?

MN   NI   PD   A
❑   ❑   ❑   ❑

5. Does the child confess when guilty without being prompted?

MN   NI   PD   A
❑   ❑   ❑   ❑

6. Does the child give excuses for unsatisfactory work?

Yes   No
❑   ❑

*"I am the way,
the truth, and the life:
no man cometh
unto the Father,
but by me."*
John 14:6

*"And ye shall
know the truth,
and the truth
shall make you free."*
John 8:32

Answer Key

Page 10

1. Stomach

2. Red blood cells

3. Blood, contracts, red blood cells

4. Exercise, bleeding

5. It recycles old red blood cells. It provides a sort of emergency blood transfusion when there is an accident or injury to the body.

6. It produces various blood cells.

7. To protect it. For the best development—all children, like boy Jesus, need a quiet, simple life.

8. Generous

Page 23

Color
    nuts, apple, corn kernals, tomato, barley, and banana

Circle
    potato, carrot, cabbage

X Mark
    cola, butter, cake

Page 25

1. See page 17, first paragraph.

2. See page 17, first paragraph.

3. They are the cells that stay in the blood stream like circulating policemen ready to be activated if that particular virus should enter the body again. They are always at "the scene of the crime" to fight a disease or invaders to the body in the case of an injury. Acting as the body's sentinels, they are always on guard. Boy Jesus must have been like them, always on the alert because of Satan.

4. *"I am afflicted and ready to die from my youth up: while I suffer thy terrors I am distracted."*

5. See page 21.

6. Teacher, check.

Notes

Answer Key

Pages 33-34

Across

1. White blood cells act like good <u>soldiers</u> in the blood.
2. When a virus enters the body, T cells identify it as an <u>enemy</u>.
3. After the blood is filtered in the spleen it is collected from the <u>pulp</u> and returned to the blood stream.
4. A special protein released into the blood that helps your body fight infections. <u>Antibody</u>
5. The rabbis filtered out the word of God from schools to a great extent and replaced it with <u>tradition</u>.
6. A <u>blow</u> to the abdomen can severely damage the spleen.
7. Antibodies help the body by killing or weakening <u>bacteria</u>.
8. A child's life should be quiet and <u>simple</u>.
9. God has provided for self-<u>sacrifice</u> in the design of the body.
10. The spleen can provide needed blood cells in case of an <u>emergency</u>.

Down

4. White blood cells guarding the body remind us of the <u>angels</u>.
11. White blood cells are called <u>lymphocytes</u>.
12. The <u>spleen</u> is a storehouse for blood cells.
13. The spleen recycles this type of blood cells. <u>Red</u>
14. These are filtered out of the blood by the spleen. <u>Clots</u>
15. The opposite of a lie is the <u>truth</u>.
16. B and T cells are <u>white</u> blood cells.
17. The color blue symbolizes <u>obedience</u>.
18. A condition that may result from a disordered spleen. <u>Anemia</u>
19. The color of the spleen and royalty. <u>Purple</u>
20. The spleen helps out the <u>bone</u> marrow when it is not functioning up to par.

Models of Truthfulness

*"Parents
should be models
of truthfulness,
for this is the daily lesson
to be impressed
upon the heart of the child.
Undeviating principle
should govern parents
in all the affairs of life,
especially in the education
and training of their children.
'Even a child is known
by his doings,
whether his work be pure,
and whether it be right.' "*

Child Guidance 151

Gardening Sheet

Lesson __Seven__ Subject ___Health___

Title ___"The Spleen"___

In Season	Out of Season
Many of the diseases of plants are transmitted only by insects.	Spend time researching how you can use natural methods of ridding your garden of pests and disease—such as companion planting.

In Season

Many of the diseases of plants are transmitted only by insects.

Aphids can transmit about 21 viruses. Leaf hoppers, blister beetles, tarnish bugs, and cucumber beetles are particularly bad as carriers of disease. Some of the diseases they carry are corn and cucumber wilt, lily mosaic, leaf roll on potatoes, Dutch elm disease, aster yellows, and peach yellows. Insect control is an important factor in disease prevention.

As you pick off bugs from the garden plans be reminded of how the spleen helps in destroying bacteria and viruses from the body.

Out of Season

Spend time researching how you can use natural methods of ridding your garden of pests and disease—such as companion planting.

Study more about the things that will make for a healthier spleen.

Removing dead plant material from the garden site will help to protect next season's plants from disease and bugs that might winter-over in the refuse. It can remind you of the spleen's work in removing harmful things such as clots or bacteria from the blood.

Student Section

"Before they call I will answer."
Isaiah 65:24

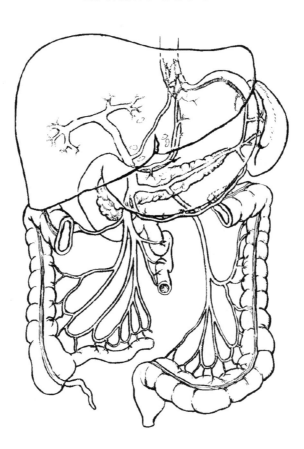

THE SPLEEN

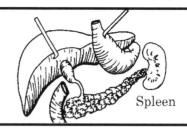

Spleen

Research
Obscure

"And that ye study to be <u>quiet</u>, and to do your own business, and to <u>work</u> with your own hands, as we commanded you."
I Thessalonians 4:11

Your spleen is located in a rather obscure* place behind and to the left of your stomach. Just because it is located in an out-of-the-way place does not mean that its role in the body is less important. The childhood of Jesus was spent in an obscure* mountain village, but that did not make His work less important. God had planned for Him to be hidden away there. From His example in this, we learn that children should have a quiet, simple life. As the Scriptures say, *"And that ye study to be <u>quiet</u>, and to do your own business, and to <u>work</u> with your own hands...."* Evidently, Jesus did not try to bring Himself into notice. During all the years of His stay in Nazareth, we do not hear of Him making any demonstration of His miraculous power. Even in His later years He sought no high position and assumed no titles.

*Hidden

Description

"...Those members of the body, which seem to be more feeble, are necessary."
I Corinthians 12:22

Your spleen has an oblong, flattened form. Its outline is nearly the shape of a comma (❜). About the size of your fist, the spleen is a very delicate, soft organ. It is actually quite fragile. To help protect it, God placed it in a safe spot; however, a blow to the abdomen can severely damage the spleen, since it crumbles easily. This can cause a serious loss of blood which could result in death.

Childhood & Youth

Jesus lived a life of <u>truthfulness</u> in His early years in Nazareth. This was an example especially for children and young people for all aftertime.

Illustration–Digestive System

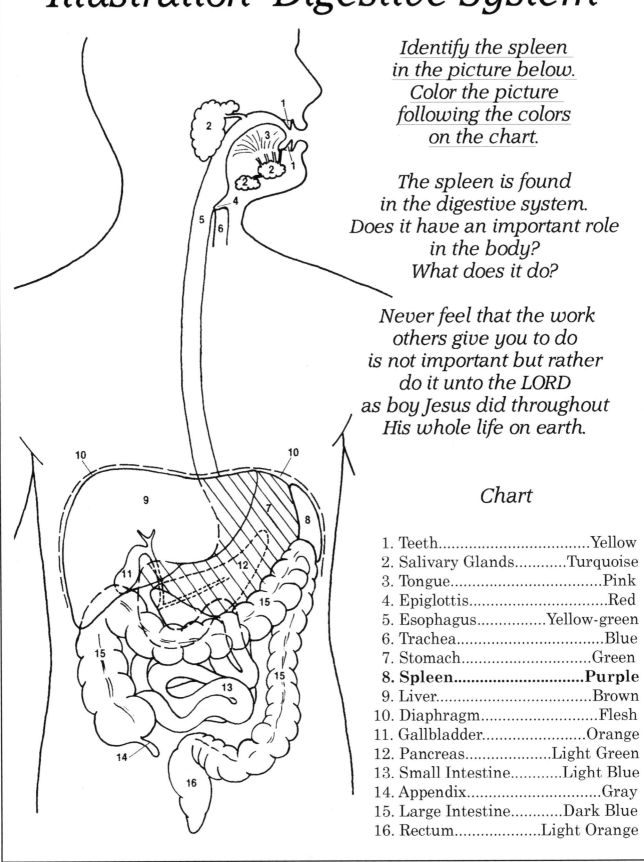

*Identify the spleen
in the picture below.
Color the picture
following the colors
on the chart.*

*The spleen is found
in the digestive system.
Does it have an important role
in the body?
What does it do?*

*Never feel that the work
others give you to do
is not important but rather
do it unto the LORD
as boy Jesus did throughout
His whole life on earth.*

Chart

1. Teeth......................................Yellow
2. Salivary Glands............Turquoise
3. Tongue....................................Pink
4. Epiglottis..............................Red
5. Esophagus...............Yellow-green
6. Trachea...................................Blue
7. Stomach..............................Green
8. **Spleen........................Purple**
9. Liver.....................................Brown
10. Diaphragm.......................Flesh
11. Gallbladder.......................Orange
12. Pancreas...................Light Green
13. Small Intestine...........Light Blue
14. Appendix............................Gray
15. Large Intestine...........Dark Blue
16. Rectum....................Light Orange

Illustration–Digestive System Information

The body cannot use food in the form it ordinarily comes in because the pieces are too large and some foods, such as fats, are not water soluble and therefore cannot be absorbed into the bloodstream or pass into the tissue cells. The chemical complexity of most food is also more than the body can handle. The role of the digestive system is to reduce large and complex foods to the water-soluble substances the cells can use. The process is both physical—as when the teeth chew food into tiny bits—and chemical—as when the enzyme ptyalin helps to change starches into smaller compounds. The timing of the digestive system is very important: food must move slowly enough so that all the necessary changes can occur and absorption can take place, but fast enough to prevent harmful decomposition. We also need to do our work not to fast and make mistakes but slow enough to do it well but not so slow that we move like the sloth (find a picture of this creature).

There are two parts to the digestive system. The alimentary canal is a tube about nine meters long running from the mouth to the anus and includes the throat, esphagus, stomach, and the small and large intestines. The organs and the glands that aid in the digestive process are the accessory organs: the teeth, tongue, salivary glands, pancreas, liver, and gallbladder. They reduce food mechanically and chemically to a simple form the body can process. We will learn more information about the digestive system when we study the large and small intentines. Whatever God calls us to do, we will pray for His assistance to help us do the job in the very best way.

We will learn about the accessory organs of digestion in the next paragraphs. The liver is the body's largest gland. It weighs 1.26 kilograms and secretes bile, a fluid that increases the solubility of fats in water. The bile ducts form a large Y-shaped tube; bile travels down one leg of the Y to the duodenum and up the other for storage in the gallbladder. A large amount of venous blood goes to the liver. The liver's most important job is to reduce or remove toxic chemicals from the bloodstream. **The spleen assists the liver by removing damaged blood cells**. Jesus assisted his parents in their work in the home and carpenter shop in the town of Nazareth.

The pancreas, located behind the stomach and above the intestine, produces a fluid with three enzymes that breaks down all classes of organic nutrients and unites with bile in the common bile duct, from where it is secreted into the intestine. The pancreas also secretes insulin from the special beta cells of the islets of Langerhans. Without insulin, sugar collects in the blood instead of reaching the tissues, a condition known as sugar diabetes. Jesus came to heal the disease of sin.

The gallbladder is a pear-shaped sac on the underside of the liver. It receives most of the liver's bile and stores it until needed, reacting quickly when acidic gastric juices and fatty foods enter the small intestine. Boy Jesus was learning during the time He lived in Nazareth and storing up knowledge to use when He began His public ministry. Today children can also spend their childhood learning information to use for God in their adult life.

Illustration–Digestive System Continued

Accessory Organs of Digestion

*Identify the spleen
in the pictures below.
Color the pictures
following the colors on the chart.
Discuss the verse below.*

**"...They that be whole
need not a physician,
but they that are sick.**

**"But go ye and learn
what that meaneth...."**
Matthew 9:12-13

Chart

1. Liver...Brown
2. Diaphragm..Red
3. Falciforn Ligament.............................Pink
4. Gallbladder...Orange
5. Stomach...Green
6. Duodenum..Dark Blue
6. Pancreas..Light Green
8. **Spleen..Purple**
9. Cystic Duct..............................Light Orange
10. Common Bile Duct.............................Yellow
11. Pancreatic Duct.......................Yellow-green
12. Aorta...Light Purple
13. Celiac, Splenic, & Arteries...................Pink
14. Splenic & Hepatic Portal Veins..Light Blue

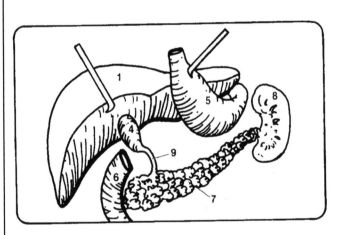

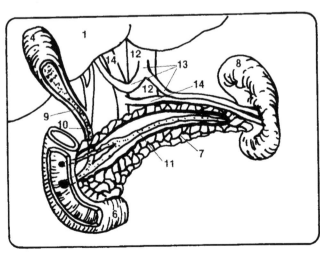

**An adult <u>spleen</u>
is about
5 inches long and
3-4 inches wide,
weighing
about 7 ounces.**

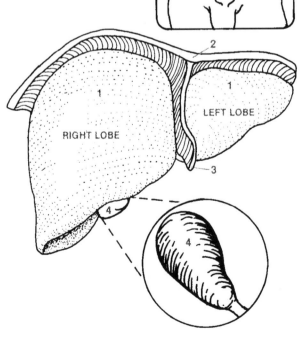

Functions

"We know in part...."
I Corinthians 13:9

Scientists do not fully understand all the functions of the spleen, but it is known that the spleen plays an important part in both the circulatory system* and the immune system. It has several key functions. Likewise, God daily teaches me about Himself and there is always something new to learn about Him.

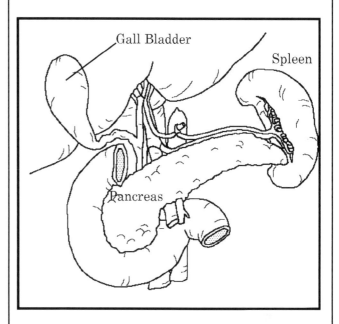

Gall Bladder

Spleen

Pancreas

Storage

"...That which is left is this great store."
II Chronicles 31:10

The body stores extra red blood cells in the spleen. Whenever the body needs extra blood due to exercise or bleeding, the spleen's muscular frame responds to the situation by contracting or squeezing itself. This action forces stored red blood cells out into the blood stream where they are needed. Then there will be as many red blood cells as possible in the blood stream to keep all the cells of the body temple supplied with all the oxygen they need. Have you ever been running really hard for a while and felt a pain in your side near your stomach? Most likely it was your spleen hard at work sending more blood cells out into your circulation.

Blood Cells

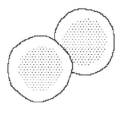

The life of Christ on earth can be studied throughout eternity and still not know all there is to know about it.

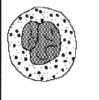

"Is not this laid up in store?..."
Deuteronomy 32:34

*See the *Heart* Lesson. See page 26 of this lesson.

In Case of Emergency
"...Have laid up in store until this day."
Isaiah 39:6

In the spleen, God has graciously provided you with an emergency organ. He loves you very much and does not want an accidental loss of blood to threaten your life! The spleen replaces the body's lost blood from its own storehouse.

The spleen is a purplish color. Purple is the color of royalty. It is made from a mixture of blue and red. As such, it symbolizes obedience unto death–blue for obedience, combined with red for sacrifice. The spleen is obedient to its self-sacrificing role in the body. Boy Jesus, Heaven's royalty, lived a life of obedience which led to giving His blood for His spiritual body, the people or church.

Grown-up people sometimes donate their own blood to help someone who is in the hospital suffering a loss of blood from surgery or an accident. Donated blood, called a blood transfusion, can save a wounded person's life. After a person donates blood, his spleen and bone marrow work diligently to replace the blood that was so generously given. The way the spleen and bone marrow work together making up the blood loss teaches us that God has a way to make up to us whatever we give away to others. He says, *"Give, and it shall be given unto you; good measure...and running over..."*

(Luke 6:38). God has provided for self-sacrifice in the very design of our bodies. Boy Jesus must have been self-sacrificing in serving others for *"...God is love"* (I John 4:8) and love always delights to give.

The spleen teaches us that God is very generous. He has supplied our bodies with more than they need of nearly everything. We could still function with only one eye, one ear, one kidney, and only a part of most other organs, but God gives us extra—more than we need to just "get by." Through the spleen, God provides us with an abundance of extra blood cells. The blood we lose from an ordinary cut will not hurt us because of God's all-wise provision for our needs. *"...Before they call, I will answer..."* (Isaiah 65:24).

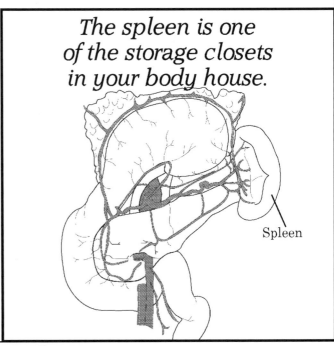

The spleen is one of the storage closets in your body house.

Spleen

"Laying up in store for themselves a good foundation against the time to come...."
I Timothy 6:19

In His childhood years Jesus stored His mind with the **truth**.
This gave Him a good foundation against the time to come
when He would be opposed by the Jewish leaders.

The spleen lays up in store red blood cells as an emergency provision
"...against the time to come...."
The blood cells are the foundation of our health because
"...the life of the flesh is in the blood..." (Leviticus 17:11).

Reviewing the Work of the Heart

"There is a river,
the streams whereof shall make glad the city of God,
the holy place of the tabernacles of the most High."
Psalm 46:4

Your heart* is a very special muscle which keeps blood moving around your body. If you put your hand on your chest near your heart, you will feel it beating. Each time it beats, it pumps blood out around your body.

Your blood is like a fast-moving river flowing around your body. It travels around your body in thin tubes called blood vessels. It carries useful things—like oxygen from the air you breathe, and the goodness from the food you eat—to every part of you. It also helps your body to fight germs.

When you were a baby, you had less than a quart (a liter) of blood—not quite enough to fill a milk carton. When you grow up, you will have about 5 quarts (5 liters) of blood—enough to half fill a bucket!

Your heart grow with you—it get bigger as you do. Whatever size you are now, your heart will be a bit bigger than your fist.

To hear a heart beating, find somewhere quiet and rest your ear against a friend's chest. You should hear two sounds close together— "lub-dub, lub-dub."

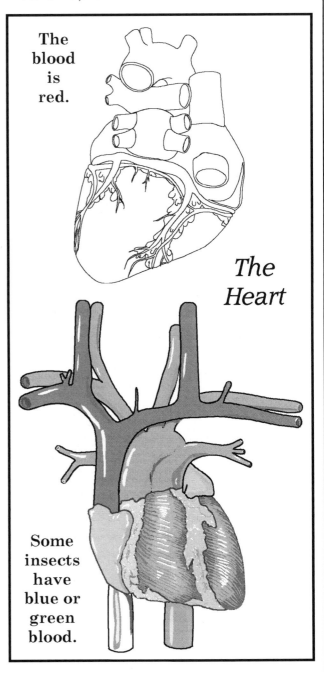

The blood is red.

The Heart

Some insects have blue or green blood.

*See the *Heart* lesson.

Filter

"...Can I discern between good and evil?..."
II Samuel 19:35

Blood passing through the spleen travels through a maze of sponge-like spaces (sinusoids). Old, worn-out blood cells and foreign substances are filtered out of the blood stream and broken down in the spongy recesses of the spleen. The worn-out parts are recycled, and whatever is still valuable is returned to the blood to be used by the bone marrow in the production of new red blood cells.

The spleen provides an example of how you need to exercise discernment about what is good for you and what is not the best. Like the spleen helps filter useless substances from the body, Boy Jesus gave you an example of how, by studying and living by God's Word, you can rid your life of old ways that are not best for you. Jesus filtered His life through the sieve of God's **truth**. He gained knowledge just like you can, by an intimate acquaintance with the Scriptures. The wisdom He revealed in His later life shows how His early years must have been given to the study of God's Word. You can determine to follow His example and live according to the principles of **truthfulness**. This will lead you to get rid of everything in your life that is false, artificial or "put-on."

Small clots are continually being filtered from the blood stream or river by the spleen, as well as by the bone marrow and the liver. A clot is a soft, semi-solid mass of coagulated* blood or lymph. If clots were left in the blood stream they could get stuck and block off the flow of blood. This could have very serious consequences.

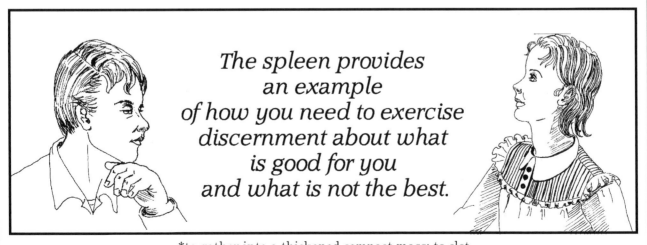

The spleen provides an example of how you need to exercise discernment about what is good for you and what is not the best.

*to gather into a thickened compact mass; to clot

Helping Out

"For whether is greater,
he that sitteth at meat,
or he that serveth?
is not he that sitteth at meat?
but I am among you
as he that serveth."
Luke 22:27

If, for some reason, the bone marrow becomes damaged, the spleen can help out by producing various blood cells. The Bible tells us about one thing that can cause the bone marrow not to produce properly. Look up the answer in Proverbs 17:22. The spleen, helping out when another part fails in its work, can remind us of the faithful work boy Jesus no doubt did to help out in His peasant's home. He must have faithfully and cheerfully acted His part in bearing the burdens of the household for He later said of Himself, *"...I am among you as he that serveth."* During His life on earth, Jesus was an earnest and constant worker. He expected much; therefore He did much. Jesus did not avoid care and responsibility, as do many who profess to be His followers. It is because they seek to side-step this discipline that so many are weak and lacking. They may possess many good traits, but they are almost useless when difficult situations are to be met.

Reinforce

Read the story,
"I Don't See
What Good I Am Doing?"

Jesus faithfully
and cheerfully
acted His part
in bearing
the burdens
of the household

"I Don't See What Good I Am Doing"

" 'We must do some good every day, and not be willing to have one day pass without this;' so Mr. Worth said in his sermon last Sabbath. I wish he had been a little more particular as to what such a one as I can do, without money and with hardly any time. I believe I'll go around by the factory neighborhood this afternoon, as, for a wonder, I can be spared, and see if I can persuade any of the mothers to send their child to church."

So spake Linda Curtiss, the eldest child of a large family, with much to occupy her at home. She went on her promised errand; but not being very successful, was returning home much discouraged, when she met the minister's wife, whose cheerful face she was always glad to see.

"Ah, Linda, it is long since I've seen you, and this is a very pleasant meeting. You've not been to the parsonage for some time."

"No ma'am," replied Linda; "to tell the truth, I've been too busy to go anywhere. I don't find even time to do any good, as Mr. Worth spoke to us about at church. Today I happened to have a little leisure, and so thought I would try to hunt up children to attend church, but I have not succeeded very well."

"Ah, well; the very intention is something," said the kind lady, who felt that the girl needed encouragement.

Linda's face brightened, and Mrs. Worth continued—

"The thought which you have bestowed upon this subject will be a benefit to you by bringing your mental powers into exercise to devise some way of serving others; and although you were not successful this afternoon you may be next time. Besides, God accepts a willing mind. This is more to Him than mere service, or than great service without the ready, cheerful will."

Where are some places where you can do good?

"Oh, these are nice thoughts for me," replied Linda. "I've been thinking, this ever so long, what good I could do, and it really seemed as if there was no way for me. I have to do my part toward earning money at home; for we're not as well off as before father died, and I have but little time."

"You do good at home, if I'm not mistaken."

Linda looked up inquiringly, and her friend continued—

"Would not mother miss the cheerful words and ready help which she finds in her eldest daughter? Would not grandmother miss the daily little attentions which seem nothing to you, but which are everything to the lonely, aged heart which has buried nearly all its treasures? These little kindnesses are more than great service, and I speak of them to encourage you, but not to prevent your doing duties outside of home if possible."

Mrs. Worth had seen and known enough of the girl's habits at home to warrant her speaking thus. Besides, her teacher at church, who boarded there, had borne testimony to her loving service.

"Oh, do you think God is pleased with those things?" asked Linda.

"To be sure my child. Everything of this kind tends to swell the sum of human happiness, and God delights in this. It is a part of the fulfillment of the '...*new commandment...*' '...*love one another...*' (John 13:34). Of what use are churches, if not to make people better and, consequently, happier? Too many have a certain round of what they call religious duties, and seem to overlook entirely the spirit of their lives, forgetting that there are such precepts as '...*Be pitiful;*' '*Be courteous*' (I Peter 3:8); '*Be kindly affectioned one to another...*' (Romans 12:10)."

How can you do good in your home?
in your neighborhood?
in the mission field?

Something For Somebody

Something for somebody! Let it peal
  Through the daybreak of the morning air.
Something for somebody! Let it steal
  As a soft echo after prayer.

Something for somebody! Let it ring
  A clear key-note through the common chord.
Something for somebody! Let it bring
  A fresh, new grace to the family board.

Something for somebody! How or why—
  It makes no odds how small it may be—
The little sweet kindness just close by;
  The lowliest duty that's next to thee;

Just giving a book, a flower, a tone;
  A cup of water to a weary lip.
Or helping the angel to roll the stone
  Out from the path where a foot might slip.

Something for somebody! He prays best
  Who lives in this great unspoken prayer:
It makes a life-song in the breast
  That even the angels stop to hear.

Life's angels listen; life's angels seize
  The something hidden within this chord.
In *"given to one of the least of these,"*
  They catch a "something" given to God.

Review
Place I - II - III

1. Choose the correct answer. Which organ is the spleen located behind?

   lungs   liver   stomach   heart

2. What does the spleen keep in store? _____

3. Whenever the body needs extra _____ the spleen _____ and sends forth stored _____ _____ _____ into the circulation.

4. List two things that can cause the body to need extra blood.

_____

_____

5. What does the spleen have in common with a recycling center? an emergency room?

_____

_____

_____

_____

_____

6. If the bone marrow is not working up to par, how does the spleen help out?_____

_____

_____

7. Why did God locate the spleen in an out-of-the-way place? Why did God put Jesus in an obscure place during His childhood?

8. The spleen shows us that God is _____erous.

Remind

1. Refilling a jar of grains or beans from the bulk storage bin can remind you of how the spleen is a sort of storage bin for red blood cells.

2. When you wring out the dishcloth after washing dishes for the family, think about how the spleen squeezes itself and sends stored red blood cells into the circulation.

3. When Mother is not feeling well, ask her what you can do to help out, remembering how boy Jesus must have been helpful, and also how the spleen takes over some of the work of the bone marrow when it is not functioning up to par.

4. When straining the lumps from something like gravy or nut milk, think about how the spleen strains clots from the blood stream.

5. When paring bruised spots from apples or bananas, think of how the spleen takes out worn-out blood cells from the blood stream.

6. Think about how you could get ready to help out in times of emergency with disaster relief aid of some kind. Make up a first-aid kit.

7. When moving about think how blood cells move in your body.

8. Go through your closet and discard or donate items you no longer use. The spleen is like a storage closet in the body house where sorting goes on.

9. Look over your houseplants or flower bed to see if any old leaves or spent blossoms need to be removed. It can bring to mind the recycling function of the spleen.

Exercise is helpful for the body house as _truthfulness_ is for the soul temple.

Reinforce
**Identify the spleen and pancreas. Color the picture below.
Read the information .**

Because a mature red cell has no nucleus, it cannot reproduce itself by cell division.
So your bone marrow constantly makes new red cells. An adult man, like your father,
has about three trillion red cells, which live for an average of four months.
When they are worn out, they are broken up, chiefly in the <u>spleen</u>.
It also stores red cells. The <u>spleen</u> contracts to release red cells needed elsewhere.
This contraction might cause a pain, a "stitch,"
in the upper left part of your abdomen or the side.
It is like when you run and run and suddenly have a side ache.

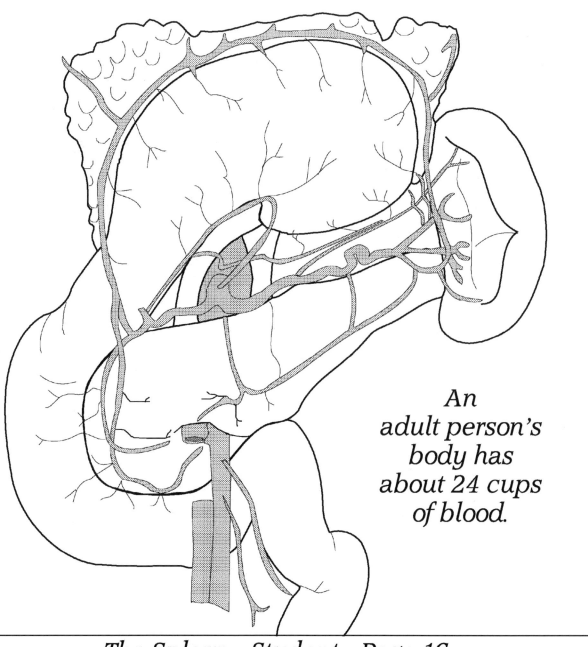

*An
adult person's
body has
about 24 cups
of blood.*

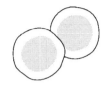

Research
Immune System

"Fight the good fight...."
I Timothy 6:12

The spleen plays an important part in the immune system. It contains clumps of white blood cells, called lymphocytes, which release special proteins into the blood. These proteins, known as antibodies, help your body fight infections by weakening or killing bacteria, viruses, and other infectious substances. About one-fourth of all the circulating white blood cells are lymphocytes. Lymphocytes act like good soldiers in the blood. They are divided into two major groups—B cells and T cells. Most of these soldiers simply cruise around watching for trouble. They are always on the alert. When a virus enters the body, the T cells identify it as an enemy and start to multiply and stimulate the production of other T cells and B cells that can fight that particular virus. The T cells rush to the spleen where the B cells live and tell the B cells to start making antibodies that will destroy the body's enemy, the virus. T cells also tell the immune system to stop when the war is over and the viruses have been destroyed. This process can cure a common cold in a week or two. It is the same process that is used in more serious diseases of the body.

Red cells carry oxygen. White cells protect your body against germs and alien chemicals.

Special T and B cells, called memory cells, stay in the blood stream like circulating policemen ready to be activated if that particular virus should enter the body again. They are always at "the scene of the crime" to fight a disease or invaders to the body in the case of an injury. Acting as the body's sentinels, they are always on guard. Boy Jesus must have been like them, always on the alert because of Satan. We know He preserved His **truthfulness** and purity. He was subject to all the conflicts which we have to meet. Therefore, He was an example to us in childhood, youth and manhood.

Satan must have been lurking around like a disease germ during Jesus' youth for it is written, *"I am afflicted and ready to die from my youth up..."* (Psalm 88:15). Satan was unwearied in his efforts to overcome the Child, the Youth, and the Man, of Nazareth. From His earliest years, Jesus was protected by guardian angels like we have. The invisible angels can remind us of the white blood cells, and their protective influence. Jesus was wise to discern evil, and strong to resist it. All of His life He led a life of purity and practiced **truthfulness** in everything He did each day. Do you follow Jesus' example?

Reinforce

Color this picture of angels guarding boy Jesus.
Read Hebrews 1:13.

Reflect

Read one sentence at a time and think about it.
This is called meditating or reflecting.

Guardian Angels

- "Satan was unwearied in his efforts to overcome the Child of Nazareth.
- <u>From His earliest years Jesus was guarded by heavenly angels,</u> yet His life was one long struggle against the powers of darkness.
- That there should be upon the earth one life free from the defilement of evil was an offense and a perplexity to the prince of darkness.
- He left no means untried to ensnare Jesus.
- No child of humanity will ever be called to live a holy life amid so fierce a conflict with temptation as was our Saviour."

The Desire of Ages 71

Christ's Example

- "The path of toil appointed to the dwellers on earth may be hard and wearisome; but it is honored by the footprints of the Redeemer, and he is safe who follows in this sacred way.
- By precept and example, Christ has dignified useful labor.
- From His earliest years He lived a life of toil.
- The greater part of His earthly life was spent in patient work in the carpenter's shop at Nazareth.
- <u>In the garb of a common laborer the Lord of life trod the streets of the little town in which He lived, going to and returning from His humble toil; and ministering angels attended Him as He walked side by side with peasants and laborers, unrecognized and unhonored.</u>"

Counsels to Teachers 276

Read the story about angels on the next page.

Angels

"Through the fall of man, the world passed under the control of Satan. Not only did man lose his innocency by his disobedience, but with it also the other gifts so freely bestowed upon him by his Maker—liberty, dominion over the world, and all creatures therein, the enjoyment of communion with his Creator, perfect health, endless life. By one act of transgression he had not only forfeited his right to this perfect state, but he had sold himself and his descendants into the bondage of Satan, and brought upon himself and them the penalty of sin, which is death....

"Not only was Christ to give His life as the penalty for sin, to taste death for every man, that man might thus be restored through faith to sonship with God, but all heaven was called upon to join in working out man's redemption. The angels were to give their service of ministry and love to aid man in leading a life of righteousness and obedience. They were to become ministering spirits, sent forth by Heaven to minister to those who should be heirs of salvation. Before the assembled host, God presented the ages of watchful care and untiring ministry that this service would impose. Faithfully He showed them how they must leave the courts of heaven for the sin-cursed, fallen world, and unselfishly minister to man till the end of time.

"Angels were not ignorant of Satan and his devices. They had seen his courtly steppings in the presence of Jehovah, and knew his subtle power, his art and deception, his pride, his hatred of all that was good. Had they not met his temptations?

Had he not invited them to join the ranks under his banner, and overthrow the government of heaven? Had they not heard his specious promises, his boastful glorying against God? And had they not seen a third part of the heavenly beings flock under his black standard, and rebel against their Maker?

"With unspeakable joy, the angelic host expressed their willingness to cooperate with the Lord in bringing back to obedience the world now under the influence of Satan and his evil angels. With Christ as their leader, who was to give His life as a sacrifice for sin, the angels pledged their loyal service to minister to man's needs, and so their part in winning back his love and obedience to God." —*Irwin H. Evans*

Blood Flow

"I am afflicted and ready to die from my youth up: while I suffer thy terrors I am distracted."
Psalm 88:15

Blood comes in to the spleen through the splenic artery which is very large. The splenic artery branches out into six or more blood vessels. These branches continue to divide up into smaller vessels. The smaller vessels empty into the pulpy inner portion of the spleen. This is the area where the blood is filtered. After the blood is filtered, it is collected from the pulp and returned to the blood stream in the same manner that it entered the spleen. The freshly filtered blood goes on its way in currents to bring healing to all the parts of the body. Jesus was the flowing fountain of healing mercy for the world. His life flowed out in currents of compassion and kindness.

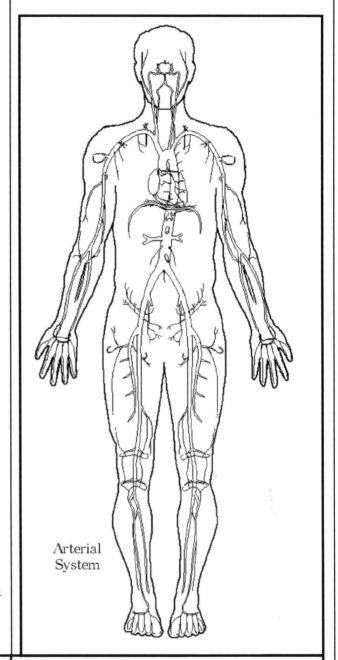

Arterial System

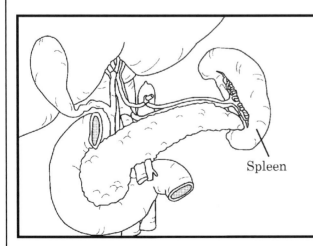

Spleen

There Is A Fountain

There is a fountain fill'd with blood,
Drawn from Immannel's veins;
And sinners plung'd beneath the flood
Lose all their guilty stains.
Lose all their guilty stains,
Lose all their guilty stains.
—*William Cowper*

Sing this Song from *Christ in Song*.

A Healthy Spleen

"...Thou shalt eat the herb of the field."
Genesis 3:18

The spleen must continually receive a good supply of blood in order for it to function properly. This is possible only if the circulation is good. Do you remember from your study of the heart what factors are important for a good circulation of the blood? Some of them are: a low-fat vegetarian or vegan diet, regular exercise, adequate water intake, good posture and healthful clothing.

Your spleen indirectly helps to build up your body temple. It must have good building blocks in order to reconstruct healthy blood cells. It is your responsibility to supply your spleen with the best materials. Some of the very best foods for building the body temple are those that God gave to man in the beginning. In Eden God told Adam and Eve, *"Behold I have given you every herb bearing seed, which is upon the face of all the earth, and every tree, in the which is the fruit of a tree yielding seed; to you it shall be for meat"* (Genesis 1:29). Some other very good foods given to you by the Lord are vegetables. God included them in man's diet after sin entered the world, saying; *"...Thou shalt eat the herb of the field"* (Genesis 3:18). The more you eat the foods God designed for you to eat and the less man-made foods you consume, the healthier you will be.

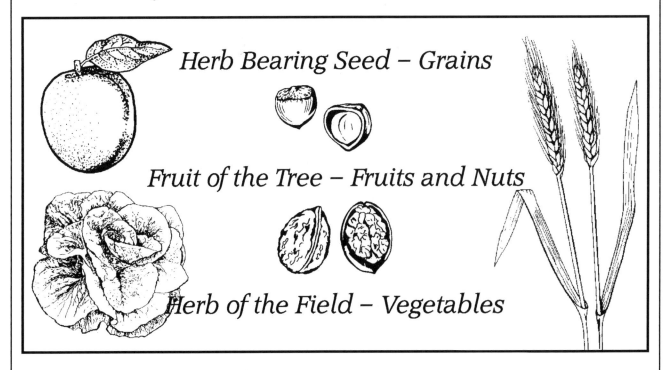

Herb Bearing Seed – Grains

Fruit of the Tree – Fruits and Nuts

Herb of the Field – Vegetables

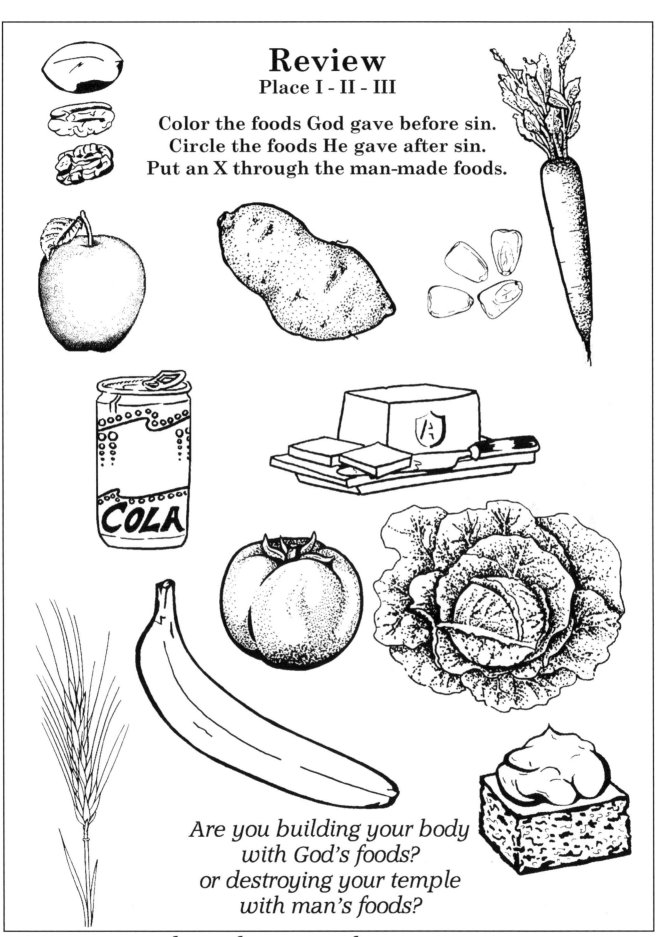

Review
Place I - II - III

Color the foods God gave before sin.
Circle the foods He gave after sin.
Put an X through the man-made foods.

*Are you building your body
with God's foods?
or destroying your temple
with man's foods?*

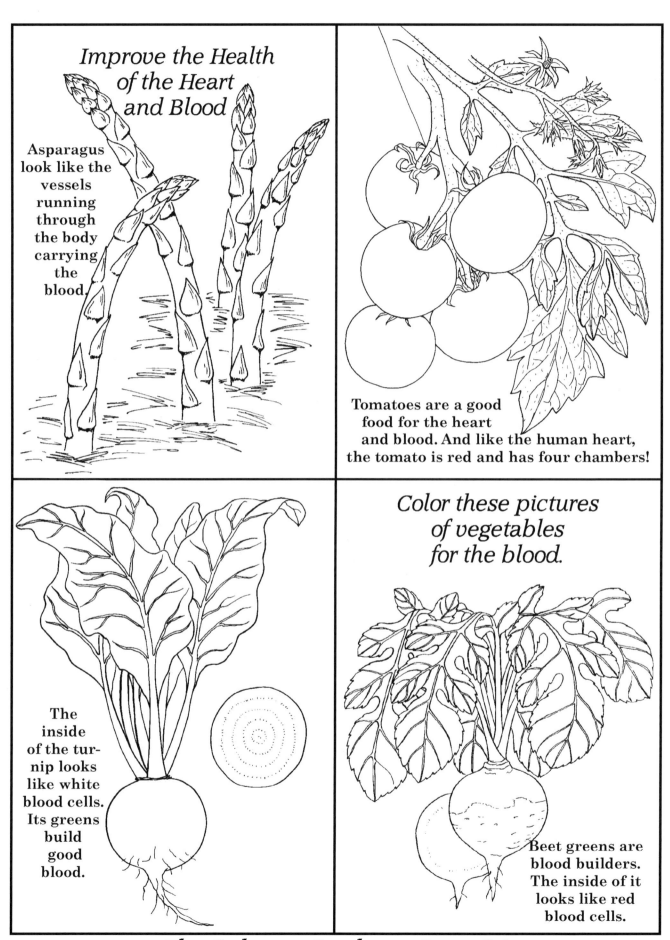

Improve the Health of the Heart and Blood

Asparagus look like the vessels running through the body carrying the blood.

Tomatoes are a good food for the heart and blood. And like the human heart, the tomato is red and has four chambers!

The inside of the turnip looks like white blood cells. Its greens build good blood.

Color these pictures of vegetables for the blood.

Beet greens are blood builders. The inside of it looks like red blood cells.

Review	Reinforce
Place I - II - III	

Review
Place I - II - III

Review (left column)

1. What is the spleen's important part in the immune system?

2. Describe B cells and T cells, and what they do in the body.

3. Who are the T and B cells, called memory cells?

4. What does Psalm 88:15 tell us about Jesus?

5. How does blood flow to the spleen? What happens after it arrives?

6. Write a paragraph or more about how the spleen can receive a good supply of blood, and include spiritual lessons.

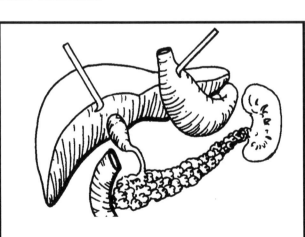

What are the parts of the body seen in this picture?

Reinforce

1. Do more research about T and B cells and their work.

2. Read books with stories about angels and their work.

It Must Have Been An Angel
by Marjorie Lewis Lloyd

Walking With Angels
by I. Lonnie Melashenko
with Brian D. Jones

Ministry of Angels
by Irwin H. Evans

The Hand That Intervenes
by W. A. Spicer

Escape From Death
by Rose Slaybaugh

3. Remember, to thank God in prayer for the angels He sends from heaven to protect and care for you.

4. Make a chart with the description of what heavenly angels look like and contrast it with what evil angels look like. Remember, one heavenly angel is much stronger than the devil and his wicked angels.

5. Use tubing and run red-colored water through it to imagine blood flow.

Circulatory System

The circulatory system supplies oxygen and nutrients to every cell of the body and removes wastes and carbon dioxide. The system consists of *blood*, which carries the nutrients and wastes; the *heart*, which pumps the blood; and a closed system of tubes (*arteries* and *veins*) that carries the blood to and from the body tissues. The arteries transport blood enriched with oxygen and nutrients; the veins carry depleted blood. The artery that leaves the heart is very large, but it divides again and again into smaller and smaller branches. The tiniest of these branches are called *capillaries*, which are only seven to nine microns wide—so small that blood cells must pass through in single file. The capillaries are the site of the exchange of nutrients and wastes between the blood and the tissue cells. Interlacing capillary beds are found throughout the body except in the cartilages, cuticles, nails, hair, and the cornea of the eye. The depleted blood moves back toward the heart through the *venous system*. First the tiniest blood vessels unite in the capillary beds to form *venules*, then the venules combine again and again until they form the largest veins. The heart pumps the depleted blood to the lungs, where carbon dioxide is exchanged for oxygen, and to the liver and kidneys, which remove wastes.

Large arteries provide direct "express" service to major areas of the body such as the brain, lungs, arms, and abdomen; these arteries don not begin to subdivide until they reach the appropriate area. Press your finger against one of arteries and you will feel the pup stroke or beat of the heart. This is the pulse.

1. Arterial Circulation...........................Red
2. Venous Circulation...........................Blue

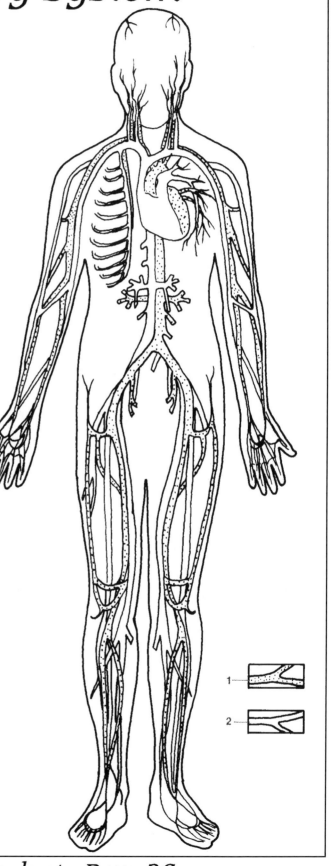

Research
Out of Order

*"The child Jesus did not receive instruction
in the synagogue [church] schools.
His mother was His first human teacher.
From her lips and from the scrolls of the prophets,
He learned of heavenly things.
The very words which He Himself had spoken
to Moses for Israel He was now taught at His mother's knee.
As He advanced from childhood to youth,
He did not seek the schools [highschool or colleges] of the rabbis.
He needed not the education to be obtained from such sources;
for God was His instructor."
[He did not attend the Roman or public schools
but attended Homeschool.]
The Desire of Ages 70*

Sometimes a person's spleen may become disordered and begin to filter useful substances from the blood. This condition may result in anemia, bleeding, or infection. The Jewish teachers, at the time of Christ's childhood, were functioning something like a disordered spleen. They were filtering useful knowledge from the Scriptures out of the schools and substituting tradition, or the word of men, in its place. Under the training of the rabbis the powers of the youth were controlled. Their minds became narrow and confined. The religious experience of the youth trained under the rabbis was "anemic." The experience which is obtained through a personal acceptance of God's word seemingly had no place in the educational system of the Jews. They put so much emphasis on externals, that they overlooked the importance of spending quiet time communing with God. They should have been teaching their students how to prepare their hearts to hear God's voice. Then they would have had a heart knowledge rather than just a head knowledge of the Scriptures. In their search after knowledge, the Jewish rabbis turned away from the Source of Wisdom. The important things of God were neglected. The principles of the law were made vague and unclear. That which was regarded as outstanding education by the Jews was actually the greatest hindrance to real development.

"Every child may gain knowledge as Jesus did. As we try to become acquainted with our heavenly Father through His work, angels will draw near, our minds will be strengthened, our characters will be elevated and refined. We shall become more like our Saviour. And as we behold the beautiful and grand in nature, our affections go out after God. While the spirit is awed, the soul is invigorated by coming in contact with the Infinite through His works. Communion with God through prayer develops the mental and moral faculties, and the spiritual powers strengthen as we cultivate thoughts upon spiritual things."*

Good Circulation Is Important To Health

Did you know that which was regarded as outstanding education by the Jews (the Greek system of education) was actually the greatest hindrance to real mental & Physical development? Most of education today follows this same pattern!

*The Desire of Ages 70

Review

Place I - II - III

1. Teacher, dictate the spelling words. Have the child give an oral meaning.

2. Do the word find exercise on page 32.

Place II - III

3. Do the crossword puzzle on the spleen on page 33.

4. In your own words explain to your teacher what you have learned from this lesson.

Remind & Reinforce

1. Prepare a kettle of navy beans mixed with white beans for lunch to remind you of the two different kinds of white blood cells—T cells and B cells.

2. Help clean the screens of the house. This job can bring to mind how the spleen filters the blood and removes certain parasites and bacteria.

3. When cleaning up with a sponge, think about how the spleen is a spongy organ.

4. When you see a police car cruising around on the roads, think of the lymphocytes that circulate in the highways of the body, always on guard and ready to rush to the scene of a crime or an accident.

5. When making bread crumbs, consider how the spleen is a delicate organ which can crumble under abuse.

6. When you have a cut that heals without an infection, thank God for the quiet, humble work the spleen does in helping your body fight infection.

7. Sing the hymns, "There is Power in the Blood," and "The Cleansing Stream."

When My Guardian Angel Talked With Me

During the Second World War my husband was employed by the Navy in California. He had not yet joined the church, so if I wanted to use the car on Sabbath I had to drive over to the military base to return it to him in the afternoon. One Sabbath while I was doing this, I was driving through a lonely stretch of country. Most of the area I was passing through was planted with alfalfa and vegetables. Large irrigation ditches bordered the road on both sides, and their high embankments were overgrown with very tall weeds. These weeds blocked the view of the fields from the road. There were no crossroads for long distances in the area I was driving through.

I was all by myself on the highway, with no cars in sight in either direction, when I heard a deep masculine voice as if a man was sitting in the back seat, leaning forward and speaking directly over my right shoulder. "Verna, slow down, slow down quickly!"

Startled beyond words, I slammed on the brake pedal. Just at that very moment, an old white pick-up truck shot out from among those tall weeds and crossed the road directly in front of me. They crossed the spot where I would have been if I had not slammed on the brakes immediately and slowed down!

The driver of the truck was apparently drunk, traveling at a high speed in a field and not being aware of the highway. Since the field lane he came out of did not extend across the highway, he did not have any place to go except into the rather wide ditch 8 or 10 feet deep between the road and the high embankment of weeds.

I was watching in terror and amazement as he almost tipped over several times trying to control the truck and bring it to a stop.

Cars were approaching from both directions, so I had to drive on trembling with shock. But the overwhelming shock or thrill of it all was hearing the voice of my guardian angel calling my name and saving my life. I cried tears of joy as I thought of the greatness of God's love shown so plainly for this little speck of humanity in His vast universe. I can hardly wait to talk with my angel in the earth made new. I hope I will be able to find words to express my deep gratitude.

The thrill of it all was hearing the voice of my guardian angel calling my name and saving my life. "Verna, slow down, slow down quickly!"

The driver of the truck was apparently drunk, traveling at a high speed in a field and not being aware of the highway.

Word Find
Spleen

Find each of the list of ten words twice in the Word Find.

The spleen helps the liver rid itself of worn-out blood cells.
It also acts as a reservoir of blood.
If a person is wounded and bleeds a lot,
the spleen gives its emergency supply of blood
into the blood stream.

```
D O O O D E D N U O W E P
I O D L N C E L L P S M P
R I O V R E S E R L I E Y S
S U O L R E A M V E R R L P R
D Y L B B S D E E L B G P L E
E N B L I V E R L D C E P E S
E E R M C E R G P E G N U E L
L S L L E C E E P R D C S N L E
B U N I D E D N U O W Y L L E S
O W S D V D E C S E E L P S E C
E E I B R E I Y L P P U S O V S
N E E L P S R E S E R V O I R E
```

WORD LIST

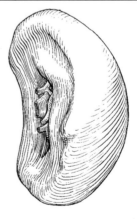

1. spleen
2. liver
3. red
4. blood
5. cell
6. reservoir
7. bleeds
8. wounded
9. emergency
10. supply

Read the story about "Transfusions" on page 34.

Crossword
Spleen

Do this crossword. Clues are on the next page.

Crossword Clues

Across

1. White blood cells act like good _____ in the blood.
2. When a virus enters the body, T cells identify it as an _____.
3. After the blood is filtered in the spleen it is collected from the _____ and returned to the blood stream.
4. A special protein released into the blood that helps your body fight infections.
5. The rabbis filtered out the word of God from schools to a great extent and replaced it with _____.
6. A _____ to the abdomen can severely damage the spleen.
7. Antibodies help the body by killing or weakening _____.
8. A child's life should be quiet and _____.
9. God has provided for self-_____ in the design of the body.
10. The spleen can provide needed blood cells in case of an _____.

Down

4. White blood cells guarding the body reminds us of the _____.
11. White blood cells are called _____.
12. The _____ is a storehouse for blood cells.
13. The spleen recycles this type of blood cells.
14. These are filtered out of the blood by the spleen.
15. The opposite of a lie is the _____.
16. B and T cells are _____ blood cells.
17. The color blue symbolizes _____.
18. A condition that may result from a disordered spleen.
19. The color of the spleen and royalty.
20. The spleen helps out the _____ marrow when it is not functioning up to par.

1. What law should rule our mouths?

Malachi 2:6 – *"The law of **truth** was in his mouth, and iniquity was not found in his lips: he walked with me in peace and equity, and did turn many away from iniquity."*

2. How long will righteous lips that speak the truth last?

Proverbs 12:19 – *"The lip of **truth** shall be established for ever: but a lying tongue is but for a moment."*

3. How does a child of the King talk?

I Kings 17:24 – *"And the woman said to Elijah, Now by this I know that thou art a man of God, and that the word of the Lord in thy mouth is **truth**."*

4. What displeases God and what delights Him?

Proverbs 12:22 – *"Lying lips are abomination to the Lord: but they that deal **truly** are his delight."*

5. Does speaking truthfully involve more than the words we speak?

Psalm 15:2 – *"He that walketh uprightly, and worketh righteousness, and speaketh the **truth** in his heart."*

6. How are we to speak the truth?

Ephesians 4:15 – *"But speaking the **truth** in love, may grow up into him in all things, which is the head, even Christ."*

7. It takes an act of the will to be truthful.

Psalm 119:30 – *"I have chosen the way of **truth**: thy judgments have I laid before me."*

8. In what way can we serve God?

Joshua 24:14 – *"Now therefore fear the Lord, and serve him in sincerity and in **truth**: and put away the gods which your fathers served on the other side of the flood, and in Egypt; and serve ye the Lord."*

9. Who will enter heaven?

Isaiah 26:2 – *"Open ye the gates, that the righteous nation which keepeth the **truth** may enter in."*

"The truth shall make you free;" and Christ is the truth."
The Desire of Ages 466

Transfusions

More than 500 years ago, doctors among the Inca Indians of South America knew a great deal about medicine. If an Inca was hurt and lost a lot of blood, a doctor would give the victim a transfusion. In a transfusion, blood from an uninjured person is put through a tube into the injured person's blood vessels.

Long after Inca times, doctors in Europe also tried to perform transfusions. But many of their patients who got blood became even more ill.

Time passed. Doctors tried to figure out why some transfusions did not work. Then, in the 1800s, Dr Karl Landsteiner, an American doctor born in Austria, made a discovery. He found that red cells contain two different substances, which he named type A and type B. Dr. Landsteiner's test on patients showed that some had type A substance in their cells and other patients had type B. Some had neither. Dr. Landsteiner named their type O.

Test showed that type A people could have transfusions of type A blood. Type B people could be given type B blood. The AB people—those with both substances—could be given A, B, or AB blood. Type O people could only receive type O blood. Yet it is safe to give type O blood to A, B, or AB people.

Why then, were the Incas successful with blood transfusions: Most Indian people in South America have type O blood. It is possible that, in Inca days, all Indians were type O. So they could safely give and receive blood in transfusions among themselves.

Truthfulness

"Everything that Christians do should be as transparent as the sunlight.
Truth is of God; deception, in everyone of its myriad forms, is of Satan;
and whoever in any way departs from the straight line of truth is betraying himself into the power of the wicked one.
Yet it is not a light or an easy thing to speak the exact truth.
We cannot speak the truth unless we know the truth;
and how often preconceived opinions, mental bias, imperfect knowledge, errors of judgment, prevent a right understanding of matters with which we have to do!
We cannot speak the truth unless our minds are continually guided by Him who is truth."

The Mount of Blessings 68

The type O blood can remind us that it is only Jesus which can give us the cleansing blood to take our sins (disease) away. It is available for everyone.

Outline of School Program

Age	Grade	Program
Birth through Age 7	Babies Kindergarten and Pre-school	*Family Bible Lessons* (This includes: Bible, Science–Nature, and Character)
Age 8	First Grade	*Family Bible Lessons* (This includes: Bible, Science–Nature, and Character) + Language Program (*Writing and Spelling Road to Reading and Thinking* [WSRRT])
Age 9-14 or 15	Second through Eighth Grade	*The Desire of all Nations* (This includes: Health, Mathematics, Music, Science–Nature, History/Geography/Prophecy, Language, and Voice–Speech) + Continue using WSRRT
Ages 15 or 16-19	Ninth through Twelfth Grade	9 – *Cross and Its Shadow I** + Appropriate Academic Books 10 – *Cross and Its Shadow II** + Appropriate Academic Books 11 – *Daniel the Prophet** + Appropriate Academic Books 12 – *The Seer of Patmos** (Revelation) + Appropriate Academic Books *or you could continue using *The Desire of Ages*
Ages 20-25	College	Apprenticeship

Made in United States
Orlando, FL
06 June 2022

18529984R00033